Scallywag

Ekphrastic poems
2005 – 2021

Isabel White

Scallywag first published in March 2021 by
Alarms & Excursions
Somerset
England

www.alarmsandexcursions.com

© Isabel White, 2021

ISBN 978-0-9565761-3-2

Printed on recycled paper by Print Resources,
Hertfordshire, England

Cover design - ink and watercolour © Laurel Roper 1970

The right of Isabel White to be identified as the author of this work has been asserted by her in accordance with Section 77 of the Copyright Designs and Patent Act 1988. All rights reserved.

No part of this publication may be reproduced in any format or by any means without the prior written permission of the publishers. This book may not be lent, hired out, resold or otherwise disposed of by way of trade in any form of binding or cover other than that in which it is published, without the prior written consent of the publishers.

For Amy & Tom

Acknowledgements

A number of the poems featured in this book have appeared in collections, journals and anthologies, or have been placed in competitions, including:

Cape Wrath – The Bridport Prize; *Adlestrop –What, You As Well?* Adlestrop Remembered, Windrush Books 2014; *Romancing the Sloane, The Garage Poet (Laugharne), Jazz Wallah, Let's Go Away for a While,* Death & Remembrance, Alarms and Excursions 2010; *Redacted,* Pendle War Poetry Competition, Posh up North 2018; *Things We Used To Do*, Guernsey International Poetry Competition 2013; *Cyd and Señor,* BBC Proms 2013; *Valedictory for Max,* BBC Proms 2017; *Frank Could Dance,* Stevenage Museum 2015; *Richie Reprised,* Sandpiper 2009.

Contents

Preface 7

GALLERY
An Inconvenience of Air and Smoke 13
Catch of the Day 14
Hireling Shepherd 15
Of Pioneers, Pomona and Peterloo 16
Nice Baps! 18
Die 19
A Sojourner's Truth 20
The Rubens Cubist 21
Geometry of Trees 22
Jesus Preaching at Cookham Regatta 23
Cows at Cookham 24
St Francis and the Birds 25
The Bridge 26
Stanley's Women 27
Night Birds 28
Cape Wrath 29
Cape Cod Evening 30
They Shall Not Pass! 31
Pilgrimage 33
Mr Turner's Contemporaries 34
Fagging for Oscar 36
Beige 37

BONUS TRACKS
Hergé 40
Kahlo 41
Saturday night at the Movies 42

LIBRETTI
Adlestrop –What, You As Well? 44
Philanderer Returns to his Roost 45
Waves from the Woolfs 46
Ted & Sylvia 48
Cwmbach, All is Forgiven! 49
Romancing the Sloane 50

The Garage Poet (Laugharne) 51
BONUS TRACKS
Please Myth 54
The Eagle Has Landed 55
Spurious Precedent of the Frog in the Nightgown 56
Joes Taxi's (sic) 57
Lullaby 58

CANTATA
Obsessing About the Maestro 60
Préludes Flasques 61
What Miles Did Next 62
As the Crow Flies 63
Lark Ascending 64
Because It's Hard 65
Saturn 66
Iris 67
Grosvenor Square '68 68
Cloudburst 70
A Tide in his Affairs 71
Dances with Violin 72
Pastoral 73
Redacted 74
Forest of Clocks 75
He's from Barcelona 76
Apis Mellifera 77
Champion (Blues for Jack) 78
Apotheosis in Three Four Time 79
Martha's Tune 80
Enmities of The State 81
Things We Used To Do 82
Cyd and Señor 83
Valedictory for Max 84
Frank Could Dance 85
Staple Diet 86
Jazz Wallah 87
Let's Go Away for a While 88
Richie Reprised 89

BONUS TRACKS
Bing Crosby's White Christmas 92
Nina Simone 93
I Know That Tune 94
Progress 95

Glossary 97
Notes 99
About the Author 107

Preface

Webster's defines a collection as "an accumulation of objects gathered for study, comparison, or exhibition". It does not state that said 'collection' needs to contain a unifying element that justifies the assemblage of disparate items. Having established a precedent with my first two collections however, I felt the need to maintain the tradition. My first collection was a series of poems that responded to loss, death and remembrance. It was fertile ground for me at the time. That doesn't mean I wrote exclusively about it, just that it added such weight to my work that it became a natural choice on which to focus my first and somewhat flawed collection.

My underlying passion for travel drove my next collection and indeed still does, though I have lately been able to direct my inspiration to a much broader canvas. Canvas is appropriate here, as my travels have connected me to art, in all its manifestations, both modest and masterpiece, and as a result, inspired many poems. How I engaged with that art and how it moved me provided the inspiration for the first section of this book.

GALLERY

In penning the poems for this section, I tried to look with a fresh painterly eye at the 'canvas'; not so much a slavish retelling of what I saw but a reimagining of what the artist might be trying to say through their medium. Sometimes this worked better than others. That said, it also provided a back story to the works which may or may not have existed previously but was nevertheless rarely shared with the casual observer (see Hopper - Cape Cod Evening).

Places, both real and imaginary, have meanings which I try to convey in my poems. They are an intensely personal response; thus a poem about bilberries picked on Pendle Hill will not resonate so strongly with the reader unless they have climbed the hill and harvested the berries for themselves. But were I to be unfortunate enough to lose my sight, I would not need to depend upon a tactile image to generate an emotional response from my engagement with a work of art. For me, the words stand for that.

With each poem in this section, I have approached the work of art in isolation, alone on the page, just as the original might be in the gallery space. For those of you who are not familiar with the artwork from which I drew inspiration, I would recommend that you acquaint yourself with it *after* you have read the poem, to see if the images the poem has conjured in your mind match those on the canvas. Of course, you can approach it the other way around, by looking at the artwork first, though this might then generate a knowing response – "ah, I see what you did there!" Familiarity may then help you connect with the art but possibly at the expense of the poem.

Beyond the fact that every poem in this section is inspired by a work of art, there is no underlying, unifying theme to all the poems and the works that inspired them. Serendipitous, they remain as I first encountered them, wherever and whenever that might have been.

CANTATA

The happy connection between poetry and music took me in a new direction, prompted by success in my first submission to the BBC Radio 3 Proms Poetry Competition, the first of two successes to date. More importantly however, it unleashed in me a passion for interpreting (mostly instrumental) music in poetry. With the musically inspired poems however, there is an added dimension. Many of the musical works featured here were themselves inspired by poems. In preparing my responses to them, I deliberately did not read the poems before I wrote my response, as I wanted to come to the music fresh. Thus, there is a certain circularity to the work – poems inspire music inspire poems, but none are alike. The music here represented covers almost every taste and style, but unlike the poems inspired by art in the first section, they are in many cases, old friends.

LIBRETTI

Sandwiched between these two sections of the book is my other great source of inspiration, the work of my fellow poets and wordsmiths, and the few poems that feature here are my wry take on their work, part homage, part observation. Of course, in some cases, I can't resist sending them up, though hopefully, I do that with affection.

As the old adage goes, you cannot know where you are going unless you know from whence you came. Thus, I have made it my business and passion to absorb as much as possible of work from my choice of the poets of ancient times to the present day. Poets are magpies, and I have borrowed unashamedly from styles and forms where I feel they fit best the work I am trying to create, and hopefully begin the process of finding my own voice along the way.

Poetry is enjoying a renaissance unparalleled in modern times. However, just as in panning for gold one has to sift through a lot of gravel, there are poets today whose work is wildly exciting and astonishing as well as beautifully crafted, if you take the time to seek them out.

I therefore dedicate this book to those poets who have inspired me most and helped me to shape what I hope is my own unique style, heavy on scholarship, constructed on the scaffold of rhyme, meter, alliteration, onomatopoeia etc., but hopefully just that little bit anarchic. So, let us raise a metaphorical glass or two to those artists of any discipline whose work has inspired these poems, who have helped shape my style; and to those whose names are not featured, but whom I admire greatly and who have profoundly influenced me. You are Robert Burns, Alfred Tennyson, Emily Dickinson, Christina Rosetti, Gerard Manley Hopkins, Lewis Carroll, Charlotte Mew, Siegfried Sassoon, Edith Sitwell, Gertrude Stein, Dorothy Parker, Wistan Auden, Dylan Thomas, Sylvia Plath, Allen

Ginsberg, Rosemary Tonks, Philip Larkin, Clive James, Carol Ann Duffy, Fran Landesman, Lynton Kwesi Johnson, Joshua Idehen, Jo Bell, Elvis McGonagall, Liz Berry, Helen Mort, Daljit Nagra and Phoebe Stuckes.

—oOo—

For the full, high fidelity experience, place your ears either side of the page, read out loud and make sure you turn up the volume!

Gallery

AN INCONVENIENCE OF AIR AND SMOKE[1]
After Pablo Picasso, Guernica

Alles in Ordnance,
Manger danger!
Goering's shock and awe geegaws
drenching these denizens of this urban byre.
Outflanked – fetlock and flintlock,
no match for equine enmity.

Grisaille beneath an all-seeing eye,
dagger mouths gape;
no escaping this *Basquaise Blitzkrieg*;
for the *führerclock shadow*, just a try out,
a little night atrocity.

Pablo Ruiz…, you do honour to your saints;
death of art measured in cube and paints, a widdershins world;
no desmoiselles, just the dark arts of body parts,
fallen angels, misremembered, from basement to casement.
Inconvenience of air and smoke;
through the eyes of Dora Maar,
on errant canvas, your unvarnished truth.

CATCH OF THE DAY[2]
After Richard Dadd, Fishmarket by the Sea

Rudely snatched from the herrings' happy hunting ground,
once gutted, my scarlet mullet,
fresh from the pan's cuss and cackle,
doused and soused, all our fruits de mer
laid bare upon the quay;
popped from skillet to gullet;
while we sail to wrack and ruin.

From ship to shawl
the kippers gather
in a "Whatcha got?" liminality of gannets and gussets.

Each glorious ebony John Dory
tells us Jonah's tallest tales,
of tiny minnows like mighty whales
who always got away;
their buried treasure,
coughed up from a sunken chest,
as any Norwegian would,
when the boats come in,
and we danced for daddy.

HIRELING SHEPHERD[3]
After William Holman Hunt, The Hireling Shepherd

And where *is* the boy that looks after the sheep?

In a drunken apple summer,
upended and imperilled,
the sheep's in the meadow;
or, jumped to the bleat,
flocks go unwatched,
while maidens, defrocked,
turn tricks under hayricks.

OF PIONEERS, POMONA AND PETERLOO[4]
After Laurence S Lowry, Coming Home from the Mill

We free radicals, well met on Pennine peat,
cloaked in moss an' mizzle;
where peewits bore witness to our seditious banter,
where we shared the poetry of labour and wait.
A Shaw thing it were, to be a pilgrim
on Equitable Street.

Thus it were, beneath those plangent skies,
I sang to thee, monsoon Manchester,
shude and shoddy, equal measured,
Tedium laudamus!

How the houses doh si doh,
Right at heart of things*
in this city of muck and markets;
yatta yatta, looming tunes,
insistent, over bridges and catacombs,
in the clef o' Canal Street and Castlefield,
girdered by mills, now stilled.

Lasses on buses bound for Bacup,
set aht for Rawtenstall;
crackin' flags in Accrington,
yon Aytoun funkateers,
wi' yer plainsong cantata of steam and sail.
I hear your waifly wail when Eccles beckons;

---

* Inscription on a Manchester Drain Cover

in Cheetham, fer a good time in a shekel and dime;
where a cap and a clog still mingle.

In seasons of mellow fruitlessness,
in terrace and tenement, Forty Shillin' Freeholders,
folk on renterhooks, peacework,
every holla, whoop and scutter,
a guttural byssinosis of jawjaw and chinwag;

I am lost to thee here, homburg and hobnail,
United and City; mad for it, Manchester,
Saturday grandstandin', music o' the massive.
Lost to thee,
at the tramstop.

NICE BAPS![5]

After Léopold Survage, Nice - Abstract

Léopold, our billycocked brohanski,
arriviste, magpie mind, beachy head.
Up alley down ginnel he sashays
to bring us his meisterwerks,
boxed clever, with raffish chips, chapeau melon.
The good Battenburghers of a nicer Nice
they would call him the lemon drizzler,
his angel cakes, served up on beds of roadkill,
figs and avocado;
always just a smidgen too saccharine.
Scene in the round, there's no hint of autumn
'til right on the edge, where he's shadowed
by that stalking wench.

DIE[6]

After Faith Ringgold, Die

That summer, the rage moved on
from Harlem to mid town,
downtown, to Madison, on Wall Street.
Now he got a gun, she got a gun.
I got a gun, I shot her,
I shot her down.

This guy ain't got no gun, got a blade.
She makin' her move, push comes to shove,
she down, he down.

Kids can't run, kids gotta hide,
they gunning for them too.
Ain't no supposin' it will end well.
No one wants to look you in the eye
now you dead.

A SOJOURNER'S TRUTH[7]

After Faith Ringgold, We came to America

We came to America, not by design
but first vacating the land, then vacating the boat,
mid ocean, our souls vacating the sea.

We came to the land where a flag lies bleeding;
pledged allegiance to poverty,
swore an oath to oppression,
surrendered our rights (if we ever had any).

Mama may sing, poppa may blow
but they can't hear, they can't know,
back in Africa,
can't hear us, choking in our chains,
our chants of freedom from the bottom of the sea.

We've burnt our boats.

The road may own *you,*
but the sea shall set *us* free
free to return
to make Africa great again.

THE RUBENS CUBIST[8]

(Peter Paul Rubens Pablo comparing Picasso with on)

Not like hourglass
Not like lard arse
Not like paunch
Not like haunch
Not like saggage
Not like baggage
Not like we live together

More like rhomboid
More like schizoid
More like droid
More like Freud
More like pylon
More like polygon
More like pivot, scaffolding

GEOMETRY OF TREES[9]

After David Hockney, A Bigger Picture

Winter reveals the trees' geometry;
leafing through capillary, vein and artery,
you're among fronds here.

A root and branch scaffold
for hard hat housebuilders,
finch and bunting, out to feather their nests.

We didn't hear you speak,
unless it was in the wind whoosh
and consonantal creak of bark;
trees undress for autumn,
a blank canvas for Hockney and camera.
We, meanwhile, are canker and cuckoo spit;
our initials carved for larks.

"Don't just do something, stand there", we said.
So you did. You have the time to stop and stare;
you wear your widows' weeds so lightly,
while winter lingers, till spring comes calling.

JESUS PREACHING AT COOKHAM REGATTA[10]

After Stanley Spencer

Swans were upping, geese a-laying,
when Stan imagined the Rhizome Lord of the River
ascending over Cookham Regatta.
This was a thing of little matter
for the chitter chatter
in their Lloyd Loom, their riverfront punts;
the pitter-patter of small fry
fretting over frocks; the flounders
ensnared in the river's locks.

What did He have to say to them,
these lovelorn lasses,
here on the river's bow beach;
to the mad friar of Cookham Manor,
encumbered with besom, paddles and oars,
and his mop headed skivvies
who abandoned their flaws
to carry their ghosts to the riverside,
the men who fell at Passchendaele
who upped and died?

I'm desperately seeking Stanley,
with his quiver of brushes.
Pop goes his easel;
Stan's fans, gorged on the rushes.

COWS AT COOKHAM[11]

After Stanley Spencer

And it came to pass
over Stanley's tillage,
here in a bosky Berkshire village,
that full frocked dairymaids,
staring at a Frisian's arse or two,
had milking down pat.
The pasture eyed babes are fisting nettles;
the trees in fine fettle for spring,
and Stanley's down among the Taplow roses
dreaming of toast and dripping.

ST FRANCIS & THE BIRDS[12]
After Stanley Spencer

Let's give a big hand for fathead Francis
conjuring a foxy farmyard spoiler
in Stanley's latest little potboiler;
corralling the waders and dippers
in his chocolate stained habit and slippers;
the pigeons on his pantiles,
the mute swans, the ruddy ducks;
this fowl arrangement
of rank and cereal number
waiting for the dove from above
to foist its grains of truth upon us,
cast down on each Gog and Magog, all agog.

While Starkadder turns his face to his boots
his missus clutches her Michaelmas roots;
meantime, under the cloche, each foghorn leghorn
gives our Fran that forlorn look.
"What's he saying?" ask the Wyandottes.
Preying for these garrulous masses
(wallet and watch, testicles, glasses)
"all hail the coming of the Golden Comet!"
(but she's here already). Oblivious, Frankie boy,
his heavenward hands in praise of the Cuckoo Marans;
here on sweet Rhode Island,
makes ready to beard his creator.

THE BRIDGE[13]
After Stanley Spencer

Jehovah's suits have gathered on the bridge,
flogged one pascal lamb too many
I'll wager; the rascals in the boat below
are navigating their Styx.
There'll be a reckoning.
On hand to capture it, our Stan
the analogue dauber,
fidgeting over every brick and tile;
he never could resist descripting digits;
a dapper drawn scruff by a country mile.

STANLEY'S WOMEN[14]
After Stanley Spencer

Grim's original dyke, our Patty,
(she'd already seen off old Schwenck
when she shacked up with Barney and the Gels).
That was before she slayed our Dot;
but then the cash petered out
and with an eye on the prize
yes, it was Patty Preece that fleeced our Stan.
Priam to his Helen, with his honey shaded bins,
pushing his pram where the Moorhens swam,
our poor benighted Stan, a lamb to the slaughter;
with barely a thought for wife and daughter,
he gives our Hilda the bum's rush.
Patty moves in, and Stan's out,
the standout painter of his age;
how he agonised over that last canvas -
a miniature mush, collared by the tallboy,
rifling her drawers.

NIGHT BIRDS

After Edward Hopper, Night Windows

She don't do drapes;
decor is perfunctory,
fawcett, cot, radiator.
Her John is on the EL,
mulling the state of their union.
We voyeurs look, don't see her,
showered in unforgiven light.
Two flights up, with a broken elevator
on Bourbon Street.
Stone heart, her mind's a loaded Berretta.
Still, there's always tomorrow,
and she knows tomorrow never comes.

CAPE WRATH

After Edward Hopper, Cape Cod Morning

Damn trees.
You mind too much your own business.
I'm made up every morning.
Still, you could have warned me!
Phones don't ring, letters don't arrive.
Nine to five I pine, and you
damn trees
are always busy,
exhausted with your living.

CAPE COD EVENING[15]

After Edward Hopper, Cape Cod Evening

Just another quiet twilight.
His wife, the pensive usherette,
a moonlit muse below the mansard,
back when sunny was blue.

Where once he lit a torch
for his old flame,
now the pooch claims his attention.
Yes, he's finally arrived,
this blaggard on the clabbard porch,
but he's someplace else in his mind's eye,
and his Rin Tin Tin is running through the wry.

THEY SHALL NOT PASS![16]
(The Battle of Cable Street October 4th 1936)
After Binnington, Butler, Walker and Rochfort, Cable Street mural

A fracas of shirts and hats,
when pious gents from cheaper rents
pitched up against the jackass, Oswald
in his baggy trousers, oh what fun he had.
The Anti Fascisti, door to door;
runners and riders from Gardiners store,
every spiv and flash harry,
hurries to the Sabbath day affray.

'No Pasarán!'

Mucho din, heads stove in,
oaths met with perming lotion,
Reg's wedge of rotten veg,
in an ocean of commotion.
Corduroy and thunder,
Mordecai's gazunder,
'Man the Mattress! Turn the tables,
all you Abies, all you Mabels',
drapery versus high street labels,
napery and plunder.

This ignominious charge of the shite brigade,
pariahs with their Black Mariahs,
all rumpus, no bravado;
and our Mayfair desperado,

(with those legions he entrusted,
their knuckles barely dusted)
hardly was it dark and they've scuttled off
to Hyde Park.

This tale is told on concrete canvas
by Binnington and Butler;
meantime, Ozzie's acolytes steal in at night,
new aliens in an antique land,
to build their new Babylon of the far right.

PILGRIMAGE[17]
(The Italian Chapel, Orkney)
After Interiors, Italian Prisoners of War

I found him crying in the chapel,
remaindered angel of the God-head shed,
whisp'ring Italian; in this, our Nissen dormer,
a whirl-without-end amen;
upfront, a font of enginuity,
un piccolo miracolo
directed by Domenico,
fashioned from loaf and fish,
to stem the scarper flow.

Roberto set to
with his fellow carcerato,
to tackle this tin thin tabernacle;
built on a bluff,
such is the stuff of the men from Moena.

MR TURNER'S CONTEMPORARIES

After Kashif Nadim Chaudry, The Three Graces, installation, Turner Contemporary, Margate

1. My entrails;
a post prandial pot-pourri;
latticed, gram-flour dinner doilies,
desert island crisp
riding this glorious tapeworm,
farting scotch bonnets.

Emerging triumphant,
from this homespun, cochineal,
gloopdroop soup dragon;
its congealed reveal -
head and shield a royal tikka,
carc'd Ibyx, best in show.

2. Prostrate beneath Queen Bess,
how the dessicate planets align;
ranged over northern lights,
Isadora and frond synchro-plummet
through red arrow rainforests,
their kamikaze beak squadrons
piercing our verdant verdigris.

3. I sit beneath your high altar
of fond and fecund pendulous mammary;
framed in a gothic bouquet,
a purple patch halo.
Turmeric brusseltops
random sadsack pea pod bosoms,
these cherished, bagged baubles -
all my Christmases come early.

FAGGING FOR OSCAR[18]
(After Maggi Hambling's Beautiful Death)

All those addled black dog days
pubbing with crispy Bacon
the St Francis of Sleaze,
or, birthing a black moustache
here, in her sullied studio
where she set
a bonfire to mundanity.

Not for her the waffle and daub.
She captured Max's misery
in the laughlines of the Wallofski Prof.
Then comes the Scollop – a giant wallop for Ben,
who (some say) was the slightest of men;
but who, then again, in his finest hour,
committed Grimes against humanity.

Godot only knows
how long is the journey of the Maggi;
how she pours oil on troubled canvas
to rescue poor Moraes from the grip of insanity.

They also paint who sit and watch.

BEIGE[19]

After James Jacques Joseph Tissot, Journey of the Magi

Rage, rage against the dyeing of the beige;
that's ecru to me and you.
There are more words that accrue to this hue
than your average Eskimoo
ever knew.

There's a kind of buff
all over the world tonight;
so let's have none of that khaki malarkey.
Let's risk it with biscuit.
It's a new dawn for fawn;
a thriller in Manilla.

If you don't know your oatmeal from your oyster,
if your sand is excessively bland,
if you find yourself swayed by suede,
if you can't help but gawp at taupe
then there's no hope for you,
'cos as Lennon says:
"Instant Korma's gonna get you".

BONUS TRACKS[20]

HERGÉ

Tintin adulation
is really so much
tintinnabulation

KAHLO

The hairs of the fair senora
Are as black as Elaine's fedora.

SATURDAY NIGHT AT THE MOVIES...

Earthquakes, tidal waves
And volcanic eruptions
Waste an all-star cast

Its Henry Fonda
He's my darling, Clementine
She waxed while John Wayned

Someone got Carter
Not many people know that
He makes bad films too

Libretti

ADLESTROP – WHAT, YOU AS WELL?[21]
After Edward Thomas, Adlestrop

No, I've forgotten Adlestrop,
forgot every letter of your name
so pronounced, it hit me
like an express train. You were gone.

You drew up your ultimatum;
I cleared my throat. You left
and no one came. Just this bare platform
for my heartache; you left me just the same.

Willows wept for me, and grass
in meadows sweet, waved goodbye;
tears, just raindrops, passing
doubts to cloud my eye.

A minute's silence rang
louder than a blackbird ever sang.
Steep was my learning;
you would not be returning.

PHILANDERER RETURNS TO HIS ROOST[22]
After Philip Larkin, Collected Poems

Larkin, about in his 4 litre R,
big ass in a Vanden Plas,
Phil's gone two tone.

Ever the jazzer,
he was Monica's chronicler,
(but oh, how he longed to misbehave with Maeve).

Phil ranged over the Dales,
regaled her with Dewey Decimal
'til she tyred of his pleasures and palaces
and lust turned to rust.

Came the day of the hedgehog homicide
Phil returned to his phones,
staved off the dust and bones a little longer;
still, wherever he wandered,
there was no place like Jones'.

WAVES FROM THE WOOLFS[23]
Prequel to Virginia Woolf, The Waves

I will arrive. I will be noticed here at the station. I am existential. I am desperately seeking Susan. I shall wear a white dress and wipe smuts from my eyes. I shall watch Bernard with increasing disquiet. Bernard pulls the legs off insects. Bernard always gets to drive the train. Neville say "hello birds, hello sky". I discard him.

I shall hate Susan for her superior demeanour. I am not pretentious. My knickerbockers are drawn together by a belt with a brass snake. I do not wish to come to the top to say my lesson, innit. Susan's father is a clergyman. Rhoda has no father. Louis is strine. He is not Mrs Hudson.

I will glance sideways at Mr. Hudson. I will wonder what happened to Mrs. Hudson. I shall be alone in that quest. I am invisible. I am an idiot. These are white words, fiery words, but I am curious yellow. They say Mrs Hudson is not real. I know different. Jinny would like a fiery dress. She is a slut.

I am a slut; I read Wittgenstein in the toilet. I have clients. Mrs Hudson is a quark. Quarks have not been discovered. I have a universe in this box. People cross over when I come towards them on the pavement. There is always chewing gum on the pavement. I shall step on it. I will stick it on Rhoda's back when she is not looking.

I am sometimes Louis. My palms are soft green. When I am most disparate I am also integrated. I sympathize effusively. I own a gun. I am not interested in Susan's white dress. I follow Nietzsche when the signals are red. I am three snickers short of my own picnic. I am taco and Peshmerga and post-modern. Mostly, I am a post.

By the way, has anybody seen Neville?

(Waves from the Woolfs!)

TED & SYLVIA[24]
After Ted & Sylvia

That morning, did those murderous crows carouse,
their prattle drown her death rattle?
Did the glowering voice of Mytholmroyd rejoice
at the Hampton darling's demise?
Fulbright and sprung from days of yore,
a filly who never set her cap
at a mardy bard before.

In that car crash of a marriage,
first there's Sylv's miscarriage,
then Assia, (the Wevill that men do).

Thunder of God!
There's so much to answer for;
those times, when life was just a gas.

CWMBACH ALL IS FORGIVEN![25]
The After Dylan Speaker (A Cynghanedd)

Dylan's propping up the bar,
with the progeny of Kardomah,
dreaming dreams of Cincinnati,
in the anarchic aroma of Swansea town.

Megan and Matti, Sketty Betty,
all the Pontarddulais girls,
kissing easy his ragamuffin curls;
and Augustus, flustered in Caitlin's bed
(while she's bedding Dylan in his writing shed).

So far from Delancey, out of kilter,
he's holed up on West 23rd;
where he will not wake, not for anyone's sake;
so much unsaid, so much unheard.

ROMANCING THE SLOANE[26]
After Peter Cook, satirist and sketch writer

Thirty years before..., the Flask...
You, yes you with your quiet pint,
you never knew
Spigot's tormentor;
gaunt and haunted,
Wisty whenever she was near,
colluding with his latest tow haired temptress,
hung on his every bon mot.

Lothario
through the window,
I spied him,
schmoozing,
gatecrashed his manoeuvres,
back when flat caps, slack jaws and whippets ruled the day,
no goons with foie gras and prunes,
to eat in or take away.

Now beyond the fringes of Theatreland
frail alumnus Alan soldiers on alone
while he's up in heaven
romancing another Sloane.

THE GARAGE POET (LAUGHARNE)[27]

After Dylan Thomas, Do Not Go Gentle into that Good Night

The ink barely dry on the Riot Act,
Caitlin lays it aside and prepares the roast.
Dylan meanwhile, holds them in thrall
in the bloody assizes of Brown's Hotel,
raises a toast while raising hell
and lays the ghost of the Bladdered Bard of Buggerall.

Do not go gentle into that good fight,
stay where the words and the whisky blend,
be oblivious to oblivion,
make free with the spirits of Manhattan and Ceredigion,
only go back when its sloe black, crow black night.

Up the hill at St Martin's,
her moniker forever faces America.
His is turned toward the good Welsh earth,
land of his fathers, land of his birth.
Just like Watkins and Augustus John
Quite Early One Morning... he was gone.

BONUS TRACKS

PLEASE MYTH!
After Homer, the Iliad

The conclusion of the Gorgon
Was far from forgone

THE EAGLE HAS LANDED[28]
Or Dan dared me, so I did

I have fallen in love with the Mekon
but he doesn't dare love me back.
He's a little green man on a saucer
I'm a little green girl who's on crack

SPURIOUS PRECEDENT OF THE FROG IN THE NIGHTGOWN

After Mark Haddon, sorry!

Driving a Coach and Horses
Through the naming of hostelries
Just like the liberties I took
With the title of his book

JOES TAXI'S (sic)[29]

How sad to see the apostrophe,
once proud cipher of possession
abbreviated to a mere plural.
Apostrophe, a grammatical tool
no longer used with any discretion,
and much misunderstood at school.

LULLABY

Now it's time to write goodnight
Time to call it a day
Put down the pen
Hang up the Haiku
Stoke the sestinas
Look in on the limericks
Pull down the pantoums
Reel in the rhymes
They have had their say

The infinitives have split now
We have to tuck up the text
Switch off the syntax
Unplug the eulogies
Apply the alliteration, (smoothly and evenly)
Fold down the frontispiece...

Night night, little words
Mr Sandman is on his way.

Cantata

OBSESSING ABOUT THE MAESTRO[30]

After Stravinsky's Firebird (orchestra conducted by Sue Perkins)

Ms Perkins, Oh Ms Perkins
I shall worship you from afar,
save your shaven fingernails
in a rusty kilner jar,
wax lyrical about your earwax
(for I have the ear of a star),
follow you home from the studio,
stalk you in my car.

PRÉLUDES FLASQUES[31]
After Erik Satie, Gnossiennes

Montant l'escalier,
nous avons découvert
votre atelier magique,
repaire d'un cirrhosist.

Pas comme la musique,
(nous sommes complices
en votre simplicité rigide)
mais votre vie, le misère et le chaos,
et vos deux pianos, l'un sur l'autre.
Dis moi, qui joue celui du dessus
plein des notes, et des parapluis?

Vos costumes velours,
les compositions découvrées,
votre vie, un découpage démente.
Un circ dans une boite, en fait, c'était vous?

Les poissons qui rêvent,
ils ne sont que vos gnossiennes,
une dance autour la vie.

WHAT MILES DID NEXT[32]

After Miles Davis (Does anything come after Miles Davis?)

Duende of the downbeat,
virtuoso Brigadier of Bebop,
fucked up Faust of the F sharp;
I man bitter.

Paris is burning and I am incendiary.
Bird and Dizzy, we three bitches shall meet again,
our hurly burly barely done.
Sequestered in a kennel full of black dogs,
dark at the end of my tunnel,
a livid mess, I am become my own anagram.

I am elemental, periodic truth,
in at the birth of the cruel.
In one more floor-mopped stack-chaired 3 a.m. bar,
way past my dreamtime,
they are sweeping up my blue notes,
my Rites of Passage.

AS THE CROW FLIES

(After Nina Simone, Sinnerman)

I ran to my young dreams, broken dreams,
a universe of broken dreams.
I ran, gifted and dreaming of Carnegie Hall.
I ran but I black – and things fall apart.
I get so sick and tired.

I ran my head against so many walls;
United Snakes, they had me blind,
and I was sick,
and I was tired.

Rallentando;
I ran to your punches,
I ran to my harm,
I ran to the names you called me;
ran to a name I never owned.

A million civil wrongs don't make it right.
And I so sick and tired,
so tired of being bitter,
a husk of a human,
the unintended consequence of being Nina Simone.

LARK ASCENDING[33]
After Ralph Vaughan Williams

```
                        !
                       s
                      e
                     o
                    g
                   e
                  h
              s
         U p
```

BECAUSE IT'S HARD[34]

After Public Service Broadcasting, The Race for Space

We chose to go to the moon
with all the brio we could muster.
To use the 'Go, No-go' argot
we rocked that airlock; then, rallentando,
we did our Far Side peak-a-boo.

It was Roger this and Roger that;
we sold our souls to Mission Control.
We packed our grip, our drums, guitars,
rollicking monkeys heading for Mars,
history writ across the stars…

Turning left, giant steps are what we took
with whitey on the moon.
Then, a little meander in our lunar lander.
Yes, we chose to go, and go back, sometime soon.

We set the bar, we set it higher.
We hoped to see our Pilot face to face.
What started out as a race for space
saw us all cross that line together.

For a while, we forgot how the songs are sung
that our careworn home is now in tatters,
and for me at least, that's what really matters.

SATURN[35]

After Gustav Holst, The Planets – Saturn

Falling through oceans of soot and cinder
infinitely deep, our carbon dates, crushed to diamonds;
girls' best friend, rich and rare are the gems you wear,
faithless gone girl of the universe.

You, my fire and ice shapeshifter, with your sidereal reveal,
what pandemonium is played out on your rings
by Madame Mayhem, my Stormzy, my Lucy in the Sky,
the very nature of things?

Your millinery of snowflakes; Enceladus,
Titan and Dione, they also serve who spin, gyrate.
Joy bringer, your rings intone -
be constant and true in my lifetime,
for neither you nor I are everlasting.
We gifted you Cassini, to share your secrets,
just to know we are not alone.

IRIS[36]

After Maurice Ravel, Bolero, via Jayne Torvill and Christopher Dean.

Always a dancer,
once, in love,
we pleated perfect.

Inviolate
as Pierrot and Pierette,
we'd Salchow, pirouette.

Later, you were my Song of India,
a personal best
in Arabesque.

When all we had left was the kiss and cry
we wrote those sixes across the sky,
perfect tens again and again,

captured rapture forever
and then, in the chasse and cherry
made history, you and I;

my cat shadowing your dove;
we were once a dancer,
always in love.

GROSVENOR SQUARE '68[37]
After Maurice Ravel, Bolero

One comes into the square. One comes into the square to meet another, who comes into the square, and another comes into the square to meet two, to become three, who came to the square and being already in the square, become the six who become the eight, become a dozen, become a score and join as one with those who came once to the square and coming now and often to the square, and meeting those already assembled, become fifty, who come unnoticed, who swelled the crowd, who joined platoons, who became brigades, who came to the square united in purpose, whose legions, both steadfast and unflinching, were swelled by numbers untold, who came once to the square, who were led by one who came once to the square, whose followers carried banners, who raised their flags in the square, who sang their songs in the square, who would not be cowed, and they met with those who came to the square who were equally purposed, who would be downed by horses, whose charges came into the square, who were also myriad and determined and who met with those already in the square, and those who came late to the square, and opposed those already in the square, would resist those who would not desist in the square, who were hell bent in the square, and the day wore its resistance loud and strident, and those in the square rolled forth, and were swept back by those in the square who pressed home, whose resolve was strong, who met with those whose resistance was fierce, and the square was filled with those who would not be stayed in the square, and all was sway and pull, resist and desist until, of a moment, when the square gave up its resistance, and those in the square knew their purpose, and saw their enemy and knew their resolve, and realised there were those in the square of common purpose, those in the square would unite in strength and those in the square would unite in compassion, and those who were not in the square would tell untruths of those in the square who were so purposed, and now of all those in the square there came of a sudden, peace and quietude, and suddenly... all the square was Auld Lang Syne...

and Vietnam.

CLOUDBURST[38]
After Eric Whitacre

I love your wet kisses,
their sudden reveal,
stealing from this ochre shroud,
the louring big girls' blouse of you,
the aspens' breathless adulation,
the jubilance of sobbing pines,
whose jazz hands greet the nation
with thunderous applause.

I love your rapid rapture,
your white-water quenching,
the gushing web-foot lashing
upsplash down drizzling drench of you,
your saturate effervescent refrains,
your sodden reframing of sheets and buckets;
the pelting, hammering, drumming,
brisk frisk of your soaking,
with your cats and dogs and stair-rods,
top down tipping.

It's a good day for absolution,
but your Monsoon's over all too soon
and that dry old prune of a sun is waiting.

A TIDE IN HIS AFFAIRS[39]
(Claude abandons Ms. Lily Texier)
After Claude Debussy, La Mer

Lily sang in her chains, rudderless, scuppered.
Deaf to her pleas, you made sail,
weighed anchor in uncertain sea;
a sea in its fathoming
of your salty shingerleens,
your mellifluous malfeasance;
you, whose sirens change with the seasons;
you, for whom the barcaroles toll.

"J'accuse!", said the sea.
You appeased her with doldrums,
ceaseless eddies and quavered staves.
With this paean you traded winds,
roared in your forté.
"Hawl away, hawl away!",
whence you harboured your desires,
your lovers, your lyres.

DANCES WITH VIOLIN[40]
(Named for a poet)
After Samuel Coleridge Taylor, Hiawatha

Spun a creole yarn from Samuel,
Afro-Mahler (son of Daniel,
coroner to Senegambia),
grandson of a Croydon farrier,
most precocious Elgar Scholar,
scored a ballade in A Minor
on the Death of Minnehaha;
sold a hundred thousand copies;
crossed the shining Big-Sea-Water.
Three Cantata charmed the POTUS,
at the White House, magnum opus.

PASTORAL[41]

After Lili Boulanger, pour les Funérailles d'un Soldat

By dint of her music
Lili stints for the boys from the front;
spectral lancers nightly hovering
beyond his bed,
as field guns pound around his head
and white ghosts come;
Te Deum laudanum.

Lili writes cantata on sclerotic arms;
calamitous conductor of this lancet band
orchestrates her saw-tooth scherzos,
conducts her curettes, her cautery of cannula
fiddle faddle, rasp, skid and splint…

At this instrumental coda
Death sutures her trenchant troops,
ripe for plucking
one morning in Spring.

REDACTED
(Alternative Telegrams from the front)
After Anna Meredith, Five Telegrams

I am quite well	I am in hell
I have been admitted to hospital	I have been admitted to bedlam
Wounded	Self inflicted
And am going on well	And am not going on
And hope to be discharged soon	And like to be dishonoured soon
I am being sent down to the base	I am being sent round the bend
I have received your letter	I am deceived by your letter
Telegram	Gasper
Parcel	Whizzbang
Letter follows at first opportunity	Lies follow at first opportunity
I have received no letter from you	I have received no hope from you
Lately	Too late
For a long time	For eternity
Signature only	You are not reading this

FOREST OF CLOCKS[42]
After Philip Cashian

In Gnomon's land
there's Grande Sonnerie,
then suddenly,
it's chatter o'clock,
tomic tickettyboo,
tock, cock and barrel,
birefringence...

No escapement from riotous dis-assembly.
In the drift of hours,
an insistent, Wakey Wakey!
We seed our stackfreeds,
temper amplitude
with brut and burnish
'til all begins to pawl.

Clepsydra still splashes,
Tompion's tapocata overcoils,
master & slave
to Cabinotier
Hmmm hah!

Tick

ff.

no time like the present.

HE'S FROM BARCELONA[43]
After Manuel de Falla, Three Cornered Hat

Draped round the doorframe,
(his cat among my pidgin)
with a smidgen of amor,
mi señor brujo invades the floor.

We wink and prance a moody sarabande,
him in matador duds,
me, mantilla, isinglass and curls.

We stir the salon girls,
and all their gooseberry fools unite
in this merry gigue;
a rigmarole Espagnole.

Buenos noches, hombre.
Hats doffed to Larry,
you broke our hearts.

APIS MELLIFERA[44]

Updated from Thomas Arne, Where the Bee Sucks, from Ariel's song – The Tempest, William Shakespeare.

Yo, bumblestinger,
humblebum bus boy,
totin' your honey luggage;
solid state pollinator,
born to graft;
mellifluous mothersucker,
far out fuzz fairy,
oh so exoskeletal,
cruisin' cowslips for bells to lie in,
no time to crouch 'til owls do cry.

Necking that nectar,
drone to the bone,
hive talkin' honeydripper,
drunk as a skunk on that spirit of the beehive,
in mighty fine fettle;
lookin' gorgeous tonight petal.

CHAMPION (Blues for Jack)[45]
After Champion Jack Dupree

Woke up this mornin',
found thy piano,
in't muddy waters 't Calder,
thee, me and Cherokee Dupree,
mannish boy of yon barrelhouse Chicken Shack,
what boxed clever,
for cook,
for country.

When we was all smudge and struggle,
thine was our Hoochie Coochie baby grand,
but we've had nobbut blues since thee been gone;
so get thee sen down't road a piece,
happen thar'll haunt stalls o' the Hall,
and lay thy burden down
in Ovenden,
no mither.

We'll not see thy like again mind,
nor Blind Willie Eckerslike,
nor yon Tampa Red
neither.

APOTHEOSIS IN THREE FOUR TIME[46]
After Maurice Ravel, La Valse

No Gallopp und Geschwind
for this brigadier und bint,
as minims run counter to maxim.

Diaghilev gives us his thousand-yard stare.
The notes connote through the gas and air,
he's late for a date with heaven.

In the throes of our coda,
its oompah harrumph,
a late reveille, a cornet cry,
outranked and outflanked,
in our Totentanz,
we salute Silent Susan
and die.

MARTHA'S TUNE[47]
After Aaron Copeland, Appalachia

Over Ripshin to Adirondack,
Blue Ridge sourwoods to yonder hick'ry,
Under the shagbark, always ago...,

he done brought simple gifts
for miss comely homely
(weren't no contrarious briggity boy),
stayed 'til laugh killed lonely.

Purtiest gal he ever see,
flash o' lace under linsey woolsey,
Lord of her dance was he.

All sass and sassafras, she set a spell,
snare him with crawdad, poke sallet, saxifrage,
rimptions of fall grapes,
"Y'all come back now..."

Nary a summer day was done
he got to be ridin',
catchin' up to the sun.

ENMITIES OF THE STATE[48]
For Trotsky, Bubnov, Sokolnikov, Zinoviev,
Kamenev, Stalin and Lenin
After Sergei Prokofiev, Seven - They Are Seven

You are Septenary, a cosmic gradation,
gods independent and supreme; daemons with fanatics,
You are the new magi, your power deified,
You are the Nature of Things.
You are that "which composes, decomposes compound bodies".
Seven, you are seven, seven under Lenin,
the Munificent Seven, who tore themselves apart.

THINGS WE USED TO DO[49]
After Bobby Darin, Things

North went the Railway, south the Motors,
Falla's Blue Bird,
Watson's grey;
ubiquitous Albion
you took me,
via the teapot church,
to L'Ancresse and Vazon Bay.

76 trombones ring in my ears,
thinking of Bobby's sailboat ride.
Fifty years have gone by.
As the tide, ebbs away;
I think of those things we used to do
back then in 1962,
when buses were always red, or green or blue.

CYD AND SEÑOR[50]
After Astor Piazolla, Oblivion

Sinuous as ever, Charisse
dips hips and slips around
her sharp suitor,
newly undone,
leg over truculent leg.

Forehead to forehead,
in practised proximity to his entreating lips,
Cyd spins,
romances his bones,
fingers bass and treble clavicle,
leg in, toe out...

Her accompanist,
Astor's abandoned bandoneón,
breath of Argentina.

VALEDICTORY FOR MAX[51]

After Peter Maxwell Davis, Eight Songs for a Mad King

I'll sing you eight songs...

Sing to a madman from over the water,
Sentried selkie of Egilsay, Wyre

Sing ma wee scoot, not yet a mistress
Beltane maid to bana-mhorair

Sing of the shrike, of corncrake, kittiwake,
jing-bang kiss of Orcadian air

Sing of a cockstride from Sanday to Stronsay
through maddening murmuration of midges

Sing of the shroud of winter frets;
of simmer dim summer, asphodel, sedges

Sing of the foment of the sea,
the tidal flow over skerri and voe

Sing of a ruckus, Orkney Wintering,
Viking longships blown to Spain

Sing Merry Andrew, you reester rascal
We'll no hear your like again

FRANK COULD DANCE[52]
After Willie Mitchell, That Driving Beat

Frank's special need was Linda
but she spurned his advances
at dances.

Smitten with love and acne
and horn rim glasses
he spooked her.

But when he heard That Driving Beat
Ready or Not, there he was,
Breaking Down those Walls of Heartache.

Frank could dance.
Still it was all too much for Linda;
she couldn't hack it,
Monday through Sunday
in his spandex jacket.
Though it was dark as night in the Marquee Club
Frank's special need would always get in the way
in the cold light of day.

STAPLE DIET[53]

In praise of Two Tone

Me am sound systematised;
rude girl in da house dat Jerry build,
strictly roots;
day after doo dah day.

Sneakin' Skabrettas,
creepin' crooks, pork pie princes,
guns feva, Baba Brooks;
one small step Too Much
Too Young.

So, no mind da Gaps,
this are Two Tone;
this are Selecter.

Godiva City Skiver.

JAZZ WALLAH[54]

After Fats Waller, My Very Good Friend the Milkman

Well all right then!
One take wonder in Tin Pan Alley,
Fats scats with coolest cats,
tongue tripped spliffed riffs,
bones nipped and tucked,
as other jazzers lucked out.

In clear and present pleasure
by turns Fats yearns and gurns,
late syncopator
My very good friend
We fell in love with you.

In swashbuckling swing, mid-take,
sweet wine of Adaline
just getting into your Stride,
its all over,
All that meat and no potater
See ya later, alligator.

LET'S GO AWAY FOR A WHILE[55]
After Brian Wilson, Let's Go Away for a While

Van Dyke normally shoots from the lip.
He parked his muse for this one;
Brian's pet sound, base harmonica,
an echo wrapped in skyscrapers,
downtown lights drawn in cotton candy
on velvet nights,
a solo in a concrete soundscape.

He whistles in some Theremin for Dennis,
for Carl.
I hear him ricochet off the streets.
No one's up,
not even the surf.

Forever 3 a.m.

Where the kids aren't hip any more,
he's home in bed now,
some dope's helmet upturned,
brimful of quavers,
minims and several bars rest.

In the Congress Theatre
thirty years away,
a windowless room,
expressionless face,
nice thought.

RICHIE REPRISED[56]

After Joni Mitchell, Woodstock (performed by Richie Havens)

It was just like yesterday,
when somebody said he was stardust,
somebody said he was golden.
On his own private Ventura highway,
as wide and as high as the sky,
the motherless child of Monterey and Woodstock
came cruising…,
tuned down to the key of E,
one chord for hope
another for destiny.

What does it profit a man,
to know the rhythm of everything
and the melody of nothing?

The child's flowers have wilted and died.
I heard them in the crowd;
they were weeping as I walked by,

and so was I.

BONUS TRACKS

BING CROSBY'S WHITE CHRISTMAS

'Tis the season to
be jolly, fa la la la
la, la la la la

NINA SIMONE

Small tribute, big voice
Nina only had nine notes
She said so herself

I KNOW THAT TUNE!

Should I drop a washer
in the blind guitarist's hat,
as he plays beneath his sunshade?
Or will he see through that?

PROGRESS

See these CDs
They've replaced LPs
(Oh no they didn't!)

Glossary

Assia Wevill – lover of Ted Hughes
Bana-Mhorair – lady (Scottish Gaelic)
Billycock – bowler hat
Birefringence – refractive property – e.g. of quartz
Breton Splasher – sweater (Fr.)
Briggity – bragging
Brohanski – brother, friend (Sl.)
Byssinosis – lung disease common in cotton workers
Cabinotier – clock or watchmaker
Clabbard – clapboard
Clepsydra – device measuring time using water
Crawdad – crayfish
Dewey Decimal – system for classifying books in a library
Duende – mythical creature – e.g. elf or goblin
Führerclock shadow – slang for Hitler moustache
Fulbright – American student exchange programme
Gallopp und Geschwind – measuring the speed of a galloping horse (Ger.)
Grisaille – monochrome painting style
Linsey Woolsey – coarse linen-like fabric
Peshmerga – Kurdish military forces
Poke Sallet – dish made from the poisonous pokeweed plant
Prof. Wallofski – stage name of Max Wall
Reester – someone acting the fool
Rimptions – abundance, e.g. bunch of grapes
Sassafras – deciduous tree with medicinal properties
Saxifrage – medicinal plant
Selkie – 'seal folk' (Celtic mythology)

Shagbark – tree species common in N America used for smoking food
Shingerleens – ornamental finery
Shude – discontent (see Shudehill Bus Station, Manchester)
Sidereal – timekeeping system (Astronomy)
Skerri – small rocky island/outcrop
Sojourner – temporary resident
Stackfreed – part of a watch spring
Strine – Australian (Sl.)
Tapocata – ticking sound (Danny Kaye – Secret Life of Walter Mitty)
Voe – a creek or inlet (Orkney Scots)

Notes

GALLERY

1. This is arguably Picasso's most famous painting. Wait! It is his most famous painting. When challenged as to the extraordinary nature of his painting and how he justified his style, he famously remarked – I can paint how I like because I learned how to do it "properly" in the first place. In my interpretation, I have tried to be true to the spirit of his work. Man, it was hard to do that! Can you find the oblique reference to Faye Dunaway?

2. Dedicated to the Beatles and Alex Glasgow.

3. You just can't get the staff, that's the trouble! By the way, I felt I had to reference Stacy Lattisaw – not enough people do these days.

4. What can I add about the tale of Laurence Lowry, now that he has been done by Tim Spall? I have to be careful here, as every time I think of his name it brings to mind that awful earworm by Brian and Michael (or was it Michael and Brian?). The actual inspiration for the poem came from an hour-long tram ride out of Manchester to visit the Pioneers at the Co-op in Rochdale (Let your yeah be yeah). It was sheeting down all day – magic!

5. This puts me in mind of Chuck Jones' 1949 classic - Bugs Bunny in Long-Haired Hare, spoofing conductor Leopold Stokowski. It has nothing to do with his paintings, however. Look out for the wench in the painting, she is easier to spot than Wally, despite not wearing a stripy tank top, woolly hat and bins.

6. Painter, writer, sculptor and performance artist, Faith Ringgold's giant canvas – Die – reminds me of Picasso's Guernica, due both to the subject matter and her sparse use of colour, except for red (for the gory bits). All her characters have eyes like Thomas Dam's trolls, giving them a startled look very similar to mine when I first saw her work.

7. It was not hard to come up with a title for this poem since Isabella Baumfree had done it for me. Faith's art is shocking, nightmarish and confrontational, especially this quilted piece. Yummy.

8. On gazing at a Rubenesque lovely I wondered how she might have fared had she been painted by Pablo (and would he have needed a model?) Of course!

9. I could not have produced this book without including at least one canvas by Hockers. I'll keep this note brief, otherwise I could fill a whole book with biographical notes about our Dave. This is based on one of his ginormous canvases of trees without leaves – well I suppose I didn't need to tell you that really as it should be obvious. Are you paying attention? Look its there! Right there! Doh!

10. In the spring of 2019, I took a train ride to Cookham, at least that was my intention but at Maidenhead the branch train did not wait for the connection from Paddington (which was on time, I might add). Whitey got all sweary as she did not want to wait an hour for the next one and screw up her day (I have to confess I used a naughtier word than that, but the man on the gate admonished me, as apparently it is not his fault, though as he works for First Great Western, I fail to see why not). Bite off the head of the chicken and the wings keep flailing!

    Sorry, I got a bit off beam there. Anyhoo, back to Stan. I wanted to track down his amazing war canvases which apparently are at Sandham Memorial Chapel which is bloody miles away. Well nobody told me. As you can guess by now, I was not having a good day thus far. All that was about to change however, when I lit upon his gallery. Ooh, what a lovely bonkers man he was (shame about his missus – see poem below). They threw me out in the end as I had outstayed my welcome by a considerable margin and it was time to repair to the pub for a roast, but not before I had filled half a notebook and bought all the postcards.

11. On reflection, this poem could be about our Patty. She had this affliction, every time she looked at Stan, her eyes misted over and pound signs appeared all over him, not helped by the ridiculous hat and jam jar specs he was wearing in his wedding photo. It seems she married Arthur Askey by mistake. Apparently, our Stan was also partial to a bit of toast and dripping, as am I.

12. My favourite of all Stan's paintings – here, St Francis – head shaped like a peanut shell – is conducting a fowl chorus in the farmyard of Cold Comfort Farm. I have carefully researched the names of all the breeds of hen, most of whom do not appear in the picture. You can look them up if you like (or not).

13. This is not the middle eight in a James Brown song, but a group of chaps who could be Jehovah's Witnesses seeing if they can break the record for the most suits on a bridge in Cookham.

14. Patty usurped Hilda's place at the Spencer table, nuff said. Her infamy knew no bounds, right from the day W. S. Gilbert rescued her from his pond and promptly died of a heart attack.

15. I always feel as though Hopper is giving us permission to spy on the intensely private lives of ordinary Joes and Janes and catching them in compromising positions. And who remembers Rin Tin Tin today? (No, not that genderless Belgian lemon!)

16. As Groucho Marx famously said "Time wounds all heels". If Oswald Mosley were alive today he would realise how ridiculous he looked in those black jodhpurs, tilting his hand up as if to say "Ooh look, here's Sooty!". The East End was so different then, especially the bit adjacent to the city, which was heavily bombed. The real estate here was valuable enough to knock down the local culture and erect glass and steel monoliths in its stead, so we no longer enjoy the delights of Gardiners store. Luckily, Wilton's (used as a field station for the wounded) survives in all its faded glory. The poem was inspired by the mural on the wall of the old town hall in Cable Street, painted by Dave Binnington, Paul Butler, Ray Walker and Desmond Rochfort. Sorry for missing the last two off the poem, no slight intended, its just that you didn't scan. Oh, and thank you Suggs.

17. Elvis would have wowed them in these Nissen huts, beatified by the prisoners from the Italian town of Moena. Now it would give the Sistine Chapel a run for its money; anything to brighten up the long bleak days of an Orkney winter.

18. Sorry about the bacon gag. Couldn't resist it!

19. Don't you miss it, not even a little bit? Go on, be honest. From the planet Anaglypta, in the galaxy of Lambrini, I bring you Tatooine made flesh.

20. Ok, so none of them are about cherry blossom.

LIBRETTI

21. Everyone's done this one at some time or other. The station isn't there anymore, but somebody rescued the sign and it has pride of place in the village. Longborough Opera is just up the road. That has absolutely nothing to do with it.

22. One very tenuous link between Whitey and Larkin is that we both owned a Vanden Plas 4 litre R (not I may add the same car and not at the same time). Both were two tone, but as I have only seen a black and white photo of his, I can't say for sure whether it was Carlton Grey and Old English White like mine. Salacious stories abound about the time he ran over a hedgehog and killed it while speeding on his lawnmower. The rest as they say, is history.

23. My fave book by Virginia. Like much of her other work, the title rarely has anything to do with the content. That's modernism for you.

24. Such a sad story. Try not to take sides.

25. Sorry! I was drunk at the time.

26. On a summer Sunday in 1972, in the crowded public house The Flask in Highgate, I squeezed onto a table and found myself sat with Mr Cook and his latest squeeze Judy Huxtable. Also includes references to sketches with his comedy partner Dudley Moore.

27. A number of Dylan Thomas's poems are referenced here – you can work out which they are for yourselves – that is your homework for today, and no, the answers will not be in my next collection, though I did promise that they would be in my last collection which they weren't. Keep up!

28. So much more fun than Bunty, but I always identified more with the Mekon. He was just misunderstood that's all.

29. Yes, sad to say I really did see this over the door of a station taxi rank. Where is the Grammar Nazi when you need her? (Cue Caped Crusader armed with a copy of *Usage and Abusage* by Eric Partridge – my English master's brother, Eric, was not the Caped Crusader)

CANTATA

30. And who isn't? An homage to the erudite and multi-talented comedienne Sue Perkins, on winning the BBC reality TV series *Maestro*. Is there no end to her talent? By the way Sue, I promise I have not been round your gaff plucking hair from the sink etc. Honest! However, tempus fugit and my affections have turned to Villanelle from now on.

31. All the really interesting words that summed Eric up were in French, so I thought I had better stick with it. He would not have looked out of place in the flower power era. I imagine him collaborating with Dantalian's Chariot or the Incredible String Band. He really did have two pianos stacked one above the other. The stark simplicity of his music contrasted wildly with the squalor and chaos of his apartment, but an air of melancholy (or damp horsehair) pervaded both.

32. Miles was an intelligent and cultured man whose entire life was frustrated by the all pervading if unspoken racism that still dogs America to this day. It came out in his music and his personal relationships. Needless to say, he could get a bit angry with anyone around him now and then. Along with John Coltrane, Charlie Parker, Dizzy Gillespie and Thelonious Monk he came to define jazz from the late 1940s onwards, and his influence is still present today. (That note was a bit serious!)

33. What more can I say about this sublime slice of bucolic England in the early twentieth century after the ravages of war. Never again! Only we did, again and again...

34. Apparently, Russia and America were not above sacrificing our Simian friends in their desperate bid for space supremacy. Victims include Albert I and Albert II. Who speaks for them today! Thirty-two monkeys flew in the space programme but apparently none flew more than once, though rumour has it one was recently in the White House (just passin!). Work that one out. Numerous backup monkeys were lined up, presumably on the basis that at the post flight press conference it would be difficult to tell if any of them had been substituted. Gil Scott Heron did not go into space, neither did Alfred Tennyson or the Police.

35. Spending too much time mooning at the planets? You can get your kicks on Ring 66. Or check out Cassini. Or not.

36. I have loved this piece ever since I first heard it, probably around 1963. However, JT and CD breathed new life into it, bringing an audience for an admittedly cut down version and proving that ice dance can be both moving and sublime. Jayne Torvill and Christopher Dean achieved twelve perfect scores in the Sarajevo Winter Olympics of 1984 for their performance of Ravel's Bolero, becoming the highest scoring figure skaters of all time. I love the idea that a little coconut matting where the ice meets the shore could be known as the 'kiss and cry'.

37. I wrote this poem about Bolero after the previous one and decided that Grosvenor Square with its insistent rhythms was a better fit. But then I thought I could include them both. Such excess!

38. I did it! Finally wrote a poem about rain that did justice to Eric's work. He also wrote Godzilla Eats Las Vegas – now that's a challenge.

39. What a bad boy he was! A girl in every port and a port in every girl about sums it up. He was no looker, as far as I can see, but what music! À la Dreyfuss affair, this is my open letter to him. (Who was this Jack Hughes guy?)

40. Next up in the earworm stakes is Longfellow's Hiawatha. I wonder if the present incumbent of the Maison Blanc would get it, despite him being a bigly fan of Longshanks. Go Wadsworth (aren't they brewers?)

41. Tomb it may concern. She never got the credit she deserved. Nothing new there then. She is buried in Montmartre cemetery, but despite doing her bit for La République pendant la guerre, she doesn't get top billing like Truffaut or Dumas, being tucked away in the second row behind a big tomb. A grave error in my books.

42. I haven't got a clue what this is about – if you know anything about mending clocks do let me know. Mine runs about ten minutes a day too fast and sometimes it gets stuck on the chimes, so we have non-stop ding-donging until I move the hands on. I worry that I will be on holiday one day, maybe for a whole week and my neighbour will have to put up with constant chiming. I could try a Haynes Manual; I am sure they do one about clocks. After all, they do them about almost anything else.

43. Couldn't resist squeezing in a bit of Del Shannon there. Did you spot it?

44. This was the result of a commission from artist Dylan Fox for an installation at the University of Northampton, and is a contemporary take on "Where the Bee Sucks" from Act V of the Tempest. As a wee tot in the church choir, I recall us singing the Arne arrangement in a competition. We didn't win.

45. Had to lead off with the definitive opening line of every blues song. Obviously, they were all early risers. Can you count the references? There are at least eleven. American blues legend Champion Jack Dupree settled in Ovenden, near Halifax in the north of England. Just imagine, those nights in the pub, jamming with the locals...

46. One of Maurice's many takes on the waltz, but this one is truly bonkers. Many of the names attributed to the largest weapons of war were female, the gun 'Coughing Clara', and the shells 'Lazy Eliza' and 'Silent Susan'.

47. Howdy Folks! We imagine Lucky Luke serenading Jolly Jumper as he rides off into the sunset, leaving a trail of broken hearts, Yee ha!

48. Do you need a clue for this one? Don't count on getting one! See what I did there?

49. Last seen on a Guernsey bus in the summer of 2015. If you go, you must visit the teapot church – the Little Chapel at Les Vauxbelets. The Music Man has a lot to answer for.

50. Astor's music made me think of Cyd Charisse, especially as she appeared in the ballet sequence in Singin' in the Rain. Cyd had a number of aliases, not surprising when you consider her real name was Tula Finklea. She basked in such glorious names as Felia Siderova and Maria Istomina. I know what you are thinking, but don't!

51. The eight songs each had themes of their own and I have tried to remain faithful to them. Eight songs for a Mad King by Peter Maxwell Davis is a monodrama with libretto by Randolph Stow. The 'songs for a mad king' refer to tunes that the allegedly mad King George III played on a mechanical organ, the titles of each being:

    1. The Sentry (King Prussia's Minuet)
    2. The Country Walk (La Promenade)
    3. The Lady-In-Waiting (Miss Musgrave's Fancy)
    4. To Be Sung On The Water (The Waterman)
    5. The Phantom Queen (He's Ay A-Kissing Me)
    6. The Counterfeit (Le Conterfaite)
    7. Country Dance (Scotch Bonnett)
    8. The Review (A Spanish March)

(In the poem they appear in the following order: 1 3 5 2 6 4 8 7). Inspiration for each was taken from the topography of the Orkney islands where Maxwell Davis made his home and where he died in 2016.

52. There are many stories in the naked city. This one is true. Only the names have been changed to protect the innocent. Featuring *That Driving Beat* – Willie Mitchell; *Ready or Not Here I Come* – The Delfonics; *Breaking Down the Walls of Heartache* – Bandwagon. There's a couple of others there too. Did you spot the soul classics (not Northern Soul – real Soul!)? Although we frequented the Marquee Club, Frank came from further afield (as in Frank Afield). Stop it now.

53. When reading this poem, it is *de rigeur* to wear a Tonik suit and pork pie hat, intoning the lyrics, all the while hopping from one foot to the other, front to back as if dancing on hot coals.

54. ~~Thomas Wright 'Fat's' Waller was a master of stride piano. Again, a number of his songs are referenced here.~~ That's a boring end note and does not do justice to him, so I will strike it out.

55. One of only two instrumentals on the *Pet Sounds* Album, this was allegedly "the most satisfying piece of music I (Brian Wilson) have ever made". Another quote from Brian refers to the poem's last line "nice thought, most of us don't go away, but it's still a nice thought". To me, *Let's Go Away For a While* is the quintessential evocation of a cool early morning (just before dawn) following a hot night in the city (to gain its full effect, listen first to the Lovin' Spoonful's version of *Summer in the City*). I met Brian in a windowless room in the Congress Theatre, Eastbourne in July 2005. He reminded me of the Manchurian Candidate.

56. Old rockers never die, they just become easy listening, but not Richie! I am just an old hippy at heart, and it looks like I was not the only one. This was Womad, 2005. I was leaning on the front of the stage mooning at Richie and when I turned around…

About the author

Isabel White is a UK based prize winning, published poet, with a particular interest in linguistic diversity in her work. She is also a performance poet, performing her work across the UK, in Paris and Rotterdam. She has worked with several universities, with a host of performance poets, actors and musicians, many of them household names in the UK. She was a finalist in the 2013 and 2017 BBC Radio 3 Proms competitions, placed and commended in seven other competitions including the Bridport Prize. She was for six years a member of the General Council of the Poetry Society and has been heavily involved in their grassroots programmes.

Her work is much anthologised in print and online, and she has two full collections and a pamphlet published to date. This book marks her third collection.

In 2009, Isabel founded the multi-disciplinary performance collective Alarms & Excursions, whose eleven regular members embrace spoken word, classical and contemporary music, dance, parkour, culinary and visual arts (graphics, sculpture and photography) presented in iconic and unusual settings, including venues as diverse as the Turner Contemporary Gallery and the Crystal Palace Subway. She has also curated poetry events for other organisations and from 2015 to 2017, ran the City of London's first monthly lunchtime poetry since the Barrow Poets of the 1970s (Wash House Poets). The Alarms and Excursions website has an extensive archive of past performance work: www.alarmsandexcursions.com